LET'S WORK IT OUT™

What to Do When Your Family Can't Afford Health Care

Rachel Lynette

PowerKiDS
press
New York

Published in 2010 by The Rosen Publishing Group, Inc.
29 East 21st Street, New York, NY 10010

First Edition

Editor: Joanne Randolph
Book Design: Julio Gil
Photo Researcher: Jessica Gerweck

Photo Credits: Cover Brad Wilson/Getty Images; p. 4 Steve McAlister/Getty Images; pp. 6, 12, 18 Shutterstock.com; p. 8 Christopher Robbins/Getty Images; p. 10 B. Busco/Getty Images; p. 14 Patryce Bak/Getty Images; p. 16 Jose Luis Pelaez/Getty Images; p. 20 Getty Images.

Library of Congress Cataloging-in-Publication Data

Lynette, Rachel.
  What to do when your family can't afford health care / Rachel Lynette. — 1st ed.
      p. cm. — (Let's work it out)
  Includes index.
  ISBN 978-1-4358-9342-9 (library binding) — ISBN 978-1-4358-9772-4 (pbk.) —
ISBN 978-1-4358-9773-1 (6-pack)
  1. Medically uninsured children—Juvenile literature. 2. Health insurance—Juvenile literature.
3. Right to health care—Juvenile literature. 4. Medicaid—Juvenile literature. 5. State Children's
Health Insurance Program (U.S.) I. Title.
  RA413.7.U53L96 2010
  368.38'20083—dc22
                                                2009026809

Manufactured in the United States of America

CPSIA Compliance Information: Batch #WW10PK: For Further Information contact Rosen Publishing, New York, New York at 1-800-237-9932

Contents

When you go to the doctor for a checkup or an illness, you are using health care. Most children go to the doctor at least once a year.

What Is Health Care?

Jamie could not stop coughing. Her mother took her to the doctor. The doctor listened to Jamie's chest. He gave her a **prescription** for **medicine** that Jamie would need to take to feel better. After Jamie had taken the medicine for a few days, she felt better!

Jamie needed health care to help her feel better. Anytime you go to the doctor or the hospital, you are receiving health care. Sometimes people who need health care are sick. Sometimes they have gotten hurt. People also see a doctor for checkups. At a checkup, the doctor makes sure you are healthy.

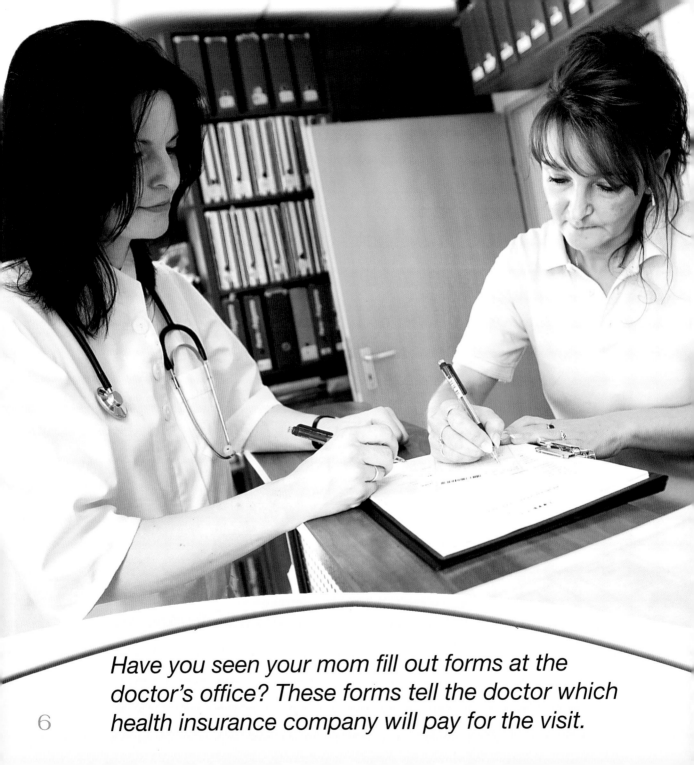

Have you seen your mom fill out forms at the doctor's office? These forms tell the doctor which health insurance company will pay for the visit.

Who Pays for It?

Going to the doctor and to the hospital is very **expensive**. Medicines can be expensive, too. Most families could not **afford** to pay for an operation or a broken leg by themselves. That is why most families have health insurance.

A family that has health insurance pays a certain amount of money each month to the health insurance company. This monthly payment is called a **premium**. In exchange for the premium, the health insurance company agrees to pay for most of the family's health care costs. Then, when someone needs to go to the doctor or the hospital, the family will not have to pay the full amount.

If your family has no health insurance, your parents may look for their own plan. The Internet can be a good place to start looking.

No Health Insurance

Health insurance is expensive. Families must pay high monthly premiums to get health insurance. Those payments are much less than you would have to pay to go to the hospital without insurance. They are still too high for many families to afford, though.

Most people get health insurance through their **employer**. Many employers pay part of the cost of the insurance, so the premiums are lower. However, getting insurance through an employer does not help everyone. Some employers do not offer good health insurance or any health insurance at all. The premiums may be too high. When a person loses his job, he also loses his insurance.

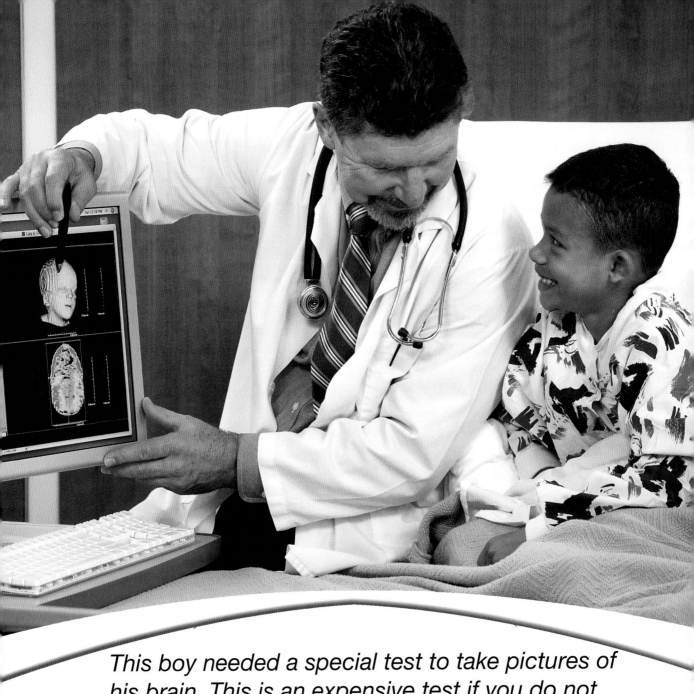

This boy needed a special test to take pictures of his brain. This is an expensive test if you do not have insurance!

Why Does Health Insurance Matter?

If a family does not have health insurance, it can be quite costly to go to the doctor. When Katie broke her arm playing kickball, she had to go to the emergency room. The doctor ordered an X-ray and put a cast on her arm. Katie's family did not have health insurance. They would have to pay the bill themselves.

If your family does not have insurance, they will have to pay their own medical bills, too. Large medical bills like this may be more than your family can pay. Luckily, most hospitals will work out a plan that lets people pay what they can each month until the bill is paid off.

Your mother likely gives you medicine when you are sick. Medicine can be costly, but your parents want you to be healthy.

Hard Choices

Just like food, clothing, and shelter, health care is something you need. You need to go to the doctor when you are sick or **injured**. You need to take medicine that the doctor prescribes so that you will get better.

If your family has big medical bills, you may have to give up some of the things you want. You may not have the money to get new toys or video games. You may not be able to go to the movies. It can be hard not to get what you want, but it is more important that you and your family get what you need.

When you eat healthy foods, as this family does, you help your body stay healthy. Healthy bodies do not need to go to the doctor often!

Staying Healthy

Paying for health care is a grown-up problem. You should not have to worry about how your family will pay for medicine and visits to the doctor. There is not much you can do to help when it comes to health care. The best way you can help your family is by keeping your body healthy. If you keep your body healthy, you will not have to go to the doctor very often.

How can you keep your body healthy? You can eat good foods like fruits and vegetables. You can wash your hands before you eat. You can brush your teeth every morning and every evening. What else can you do to keep yourself healthy?

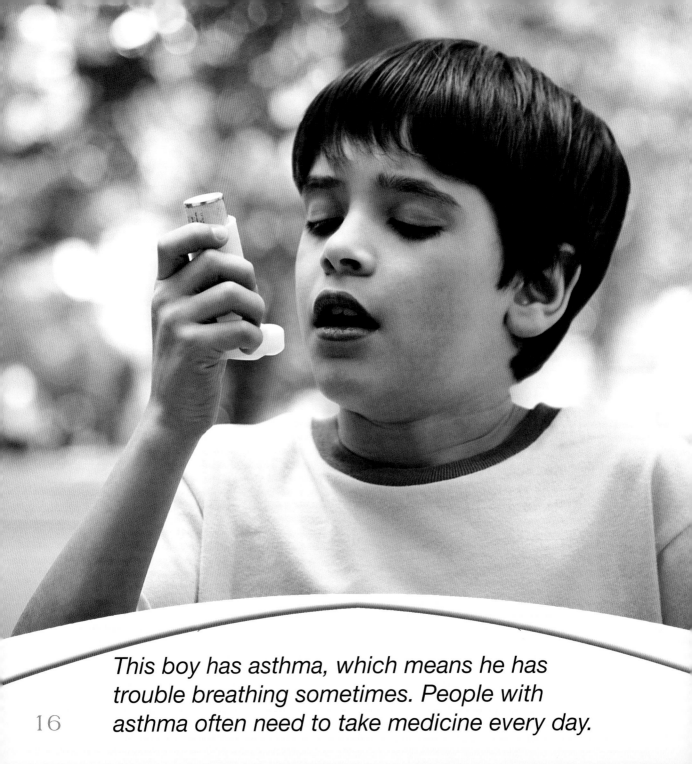

This boy has asthma, which means he has trouble breathing sometimes. People with asthma often need to take medicine every day.

When You Have a Health Problem

Even if you keep your body healthy, you will still get sick sometimes. You might also have a **chronic** health problem. That means that you have a health problem that does not go away. Many kids have asthma, ADHD, diabetes, or other health problems. Kids with chronic health problems may need to take prescription medications every day and see the doctor often.

Even if you know your family is having trouble paying for health care, do not worry! There are special programs that help people who have chronic illnesses. Through these programs, your family may get medicine and doctor visits at a lower cost, or these things may even be free.

CHIP can sometimes pay for dentist visits or glasses. Keeping your teeth healthy is an important part of keeping your body healthy.

Medicaid and CHIP

Medicaid is a government health insurance program. Medicaid is a way for people without much money to get health insurance. Medicaid helps some children. However, Medicaid does not help every child. To fix this problem, the **government** started another program called CHIP. CHIP stands for Children's Health Insurance Program.

Each state has its own rules about who can get Medicaid and CHIP. If your family gets Medicaid or CHIP, it will pay for many of your health care costs. It will pay for doctor and hospital visits, **immunizations**, and prescription medicines. These programs help many people. Maybe they can help your family, too!

There may be a health center for uninsured people near your home. A health center is just like any other doctor's office, only cheaper!

Other Ways to Get Help

If your family does not have health insurance, you can still get the health care you need. The government runs health centers for people who do not have insurance. These centers charge only what your family can afford to pay.

Many other **clinics**, hospitals, and doctors' offices provide health care at a lower cost to people who cannot pay the full amount. There are also **charities**, churches, and other groups that run clinics or can help with health care costs. There is no need to feel **embarrassed** if your family needs to ask for help. Your parents are doing what is best for you and your family.

Healthy Today, Healthy Tomorrow

If you are feeling worried about your health care, it may help to talk to your parents or another adult that you trust. An adult can explain things about how your family gets health care. Talking about your feelings can help you feel better.

Everyone should have good health care, but it is very important for children to have good health care. Your body is still growing. Your family might be struggling to find and to pay for health care. That can be hard, but it is important that you get the health care you need. Strong, healthy children grow into healthy adults.

Glossary

afford (uh-FAWRD) To have enough money to pay for something.

charities (CHER-uh-teez) Groups that give help to the needy.

chronic (KRO-nik) Something that does not go away.

clinics (KLIH-niks) Places where people can get medical care.

embarrassed (em-BAR-usd) Feeling shamed or uneasy.

employer (im-PLOY-er) A person or a business that hires one or more people to work.

expensive (ik-SPENT-siv) Costing a lot of money.

government (GUH-vern-mint) The people who make laws and run a state or a country.

immunizations (ih-myuh-nuh-ZAY-shunz) Shots that keep a person from getting sick.

injured (IN-jurd) Harmed or hurt.

medicine (MEH-duh-sin) A drug that a doctor gives you to help fight illness.

premium (PREE-me-um) Payment for insurance.

prescription (prih-SKRIP-shun) An order for a type of drug.

Index

Web Sites

Due to the changing nature of Internet links, PowerKids Press has developed an online list of Web sites related to the subject of this book. This site is updated regularly. Please use this link to access the list:

www.powerkidslinks.com/lwio/health/